DEAD HANDS

T0347806

Howard Barker

DEAD HANDS

OBERON BOOKS
LONDON

First published in 2004 by Oberon Books Ltd.

Electronic edition published in 2012

Oberon Books Ltd.
521 Caledonian Road, London N7 9RH
Tel: 020 7607 3637 / Fax: 020 7607 3629
e-mail: info@oberonbooks.com
www.oberonbooks.com

Copyright © Howard Barker 2004

Howard Barker is hereby identified as author of this play in
accordance with section 77 of the Copyright, Designs and Patents Act
1988. The author has asserted his moral rights.

All rights whatsoever in this work are strictly reserved and applica-
tion for performance etc. should be made before commencement of
rehearsal to Judy Daish Associates Ltd, 2 St Charles Place, London
W10 6EG. No performance may be given unless a licence has been
obtained, and no alterations may be made in the title or the text of the
play without the author's prior written consent.

You may not copy, store, distribute, transmit, reproduce or otherwise make available this publication (or any part of it) in any
form, or binding or by any means (print, electronic, digital, opti-
cal, mechanical, photocopying, recording or otherwise), without
the prior written permission of the publisher. Any person who
does any unauthorized act in relation to this publication may be
liable to criminal prosecution and civil claims for damages.

Cover image: Jean-Paul Malakoff

A catalogue record for this book is available from the British Library.

PB ISBN: 978-1-84002-464-7

Digital ISBN: 978-1-84943-364-8

Visit www.oberonbooks.com to read more about all our books
and to buy them. You will also find features, author interviews and
news of any author events, and you can sign up for e-newsletters
so that you're always first to hear about our new releases.

Characters

EFF
a man bereaved

ISTVAN
his brother

SOPRON
a widowed mistress

Dead Hands was first performed at The Door at Birmingham Rep on 15 October 2004 with the following cast:

EFF, Justin Avoth

SOPRON, Biddy Wells

ISTVAN, Chris Moran

Director, Howard Barker

Designer, Tomas Leipzig

Costume Designer, Billie Kaiser

Lighting Designer, Helen Morley

Sound Designer, Paul Bull

An open coffin on a table. A man enters.

EFF: What a journey
  (*He sits.*)
  What a journey oh
  (*Pause.*)
  What a journey let us begin with things of little or no
  consequence the weather for example
  (*Pause.*)
  The weather which characterized this journey was
  unremittingly
  (*Pause.*)
  No
  No
  No it did remit on leaving somewhere the unremitting
  vileness ceased the road began to steam in glaring sunshine
  birds became vociferous insects swarmed
  (*Pause.*)
  This was the only instance of alleviation I recall otherwise
  (*Pause.*)
  A vile journey
  (*Pause.*)
  Your mistress what a look she has I met her on the stairs
  this little mouth and hands which dart from here to there
  her neck her thighs her hair hands like an infant's old but
  infantile
  (*Pause.*)
  Infantile but aged hands immediately I knew I'd sleep with
  her if not today tomorrow
  (*Pause.*)
  What a look however
  (*Pause.*)
  Cruel is not the word
  Flint
  Brick
  Broken glass for eyes
  I looked away I could not tolerate her stare I blushed I
  muttered shifting my weight from one foot to the other I
  wanted her whole cunt in my mouth the flesh the fluid and
  the hair stiff hair I imagined and if she pissed so much the

7

better she said we were united in our grief
(*Pause.*)
What grief
(*Pause.*)
What grief
(*Pause.*)
In what grief united if she comes in now I'll drag her skirt
over her thighs lean lean on my father's corpse while I
(*Pause.*)
Grief is not a river is it sometimes the riverbed is dry years
might elapse before the rain arrives you might be laughing
in a public place when the storm bursts
(*Pause. He rises from the chair.*)
Or never
Never
Ever
Grieve
At
All
(*Pause.*)
She won't come in
(*Pause.*)
She won't
(*Pause.*)
She won't come in
(*Pause. He sits.*)
Despite the profoundly mischievous impression she
conveyed I think it most unlikely she would intrude upon a
moment of such tenderness as this
(*Pause.*)
Marching in here naked for example
(*Pause.*)
Marching in here naked but for shoes
(*Pause.*)
Such an act for all its exquisite insolence must be
contemplated in the context of her reputation
(*Pause.*)
What is her reputation?

(*Pause.*)
Her reputation might in any case be one she longs to lose
the discreet how they dream of indiscretion the flagrant
how they wish they could disguise their brutal moves
(*Pause.*)
On the other hand
(*Pause.*)
On the other hand
(*Pause.*)
Do you mind this do you mind this incorrigible speculation
it comes from you of all the many gifts bestowed on me
by you this mode of argument is the most precious if
argument itself is precious one might dispute its value
possibly I don't however I don't dispute it on the other
hand I don't dispute it at all on the other hand on the
other hand is it not the tragedy of women that they are
obliged to weigh the pleasures of an inspiration against the
mounting sarcasm of a contemptuous world breathtaking
magnificent religious religious yes religious as it would be
to march in here now naked but for shoes can she avoid
reflecting on the possibility that passing time would render
such an apotheosis of her sexuality comic absurd or even I
flinch from speaking the word even
(*Pause.*)
Grotesque possibly?
(*He rises suddenly.*)
She's coming
She's coming
She
(*Pause.*)
Ha
(*He shakes his head.*)
Ha
(*He sits.*)
Ha
(*He sits shaking his head.*)
I'm alone
In the world and in my imagination

Utterly
Utterly
I blame you
Utterly
Blame and thank you simultaneously
Utterly
Alone
Father
(*Pause.*)
Father
(*Pause.*)
Funny word
(*He rises and walks.*)
Rather than attending on her whim rather than passively
anticipating an action she almost certainly has never even
contemplated let alone possesses the courage to perform
might not I
(*Pause.*)
Father
(*Pause.*)
Funny word
(*Pause.*)
Fling back the door and calling down the stairs say
(*He shrugs.*)
Say what?
Say nothing do not say utter utter rather utter the appalling
words
Naked
In
Shoes
(*Pause.*)
Funny word father because like the word God God who
also was a father God who lacked the woman but still
assumed the title like God father is a word the speaking
of which induces in me why this should be I don't know a
certain nausea I enquired of my colleagues at the university
I call them colleagues I cannot call them friends if they
experienced a similar disgust in uttering this word none did

and whilst all confessed to feelings of rage resentment or
hostility in contemplating the individual to whom the word
referred they claimed the word itself was not the cause so
once again I found myself not only isolated but the object
of pity and contempt I prefer the army to the university
paradoxically the army is less critical of
(*A woman enters, naked beneath a coat. She walks to the coffin.
She leans across it as if stricken with grief. The coat slips from her
shoulders. Pause.*)
My brother
(*Pause.*)
How typical of my brother not to be here and he lives
streets away whereas I I who have every reason to be late
or absent altogether I subject myself to the exigencies of
a journey of unremitting no not unremitting it did remit
on leaving somewhere the unremitting vileness ceased
the road began to steam in glaring sunshine birds became
vociferous insects swarmed all the same
(*Pause.*)
A vile journey and he was I don't hesitate to say so the
favourite son oh yes the favourite which explains perhaps
this negligence this peculiar complacency I don't criticize
(*He sits. The woman weeps.*)
I don't because
(*She wails. She subsides.*)
If a single individual might be exempted from such
judgement as one universally applies that individual surely
ought to be
(*She sobs.*)
Your brother
(*Pause.*)
Or is that sentimental is that the flawed and perverse
reasoning which seems always to prevail in matters of the
family I don't know I'm just talking
(*Pause.*)
SOPRON: All my gestures
(*She plucks up the coat.*)
Every one

(*Pause.*)

Hang in the air

(*She holds the coat.*)

Like smoke he said he called smoke perfect and when he
smoked he smoked only to make smoke dust also he found
beautiful its drifting its disintegration in the breeze shellfire
even demolition and clouds obviously is it necessary to
mention clouds these he sat for hours scrutinizing be
smoke always he said to me by which he meant take on
the shape of others surely be formed by them concede be
moved as smoke is by the air

(*She slips on the coat.*)

I try

(*She stares at EFF.*)

I try

I try

I try to move in other people's airs

(*Pause. She averts her gaze.*)

What if there is no air however I never asked him this I
never asked him anything at all all he uttered I received as
science I received as law something in the way he looked
made every statement irrefutable even the poorest shadow
of a doubt I did not dare articulate

(*Pause.*)

Not from fear

(*Pause.*)

I never feared him but how easily he bruised a look of
incomprehension or possibly just because I failed to hear
would make him shrink with disappointment he frowned
he paled and I who had never entertained the slightest
wish to contradict him I felt ashamed I felt

(*Pause.*)

The shame a mother feels who accidentally treads on her
own child

(*Pause.*)

I have no children

(*Pause.*)

He offered me a child

(*Pause.*)

I say a child two three half a dozen children if I wanted
them he did not think a woman should be denied the
ecstasy of motherhood I myself denied it

(*Pause.*)

Underneath this coat I'm naked naked as you have
observed and whilst observing it has yet to stimulate in
you some visible reaction I am sufficiently versed in male
modesty to know your stillness might be a stillness born
not of antipathy but wonder delicacy even fear believe me
when I say how greatly I prefer the darker ways of love if
I myself have been in this one instance bright white with
impatience and

(*Pause.*)

Your brother's here

(*EFF rises swiftly to his feet.*)

Quick take my whole cunt in your mouth the flesh the fluid
and the so-stiff hair and if I piss so much the better

(*She opens her coat.*)

Quick I said

(*EFF fails to move.*)

Be quick your brother's here

(*EFF is motionless, staring at her. SOPRON allows the coat to
fall closed and strides out. Pause.*)

EFF: I was constrained

(*Pause.*)

Much as I

Powerful as my

Awful as the

(*Pause.*)

Still I was constrained and the thing that constrained me
was an overwhelming sense that far from being an act
of spontaneous desire or even mischief on her part this
proposition was the enactment of some sordid and corrupt
conspiracy between a dead man and his mistress an erotic
contract which would have reduced me to the status of an
instrument played by a man nearly if not literally in the
grave what sort of father what sort of how I hate that word

what sort of
(*Pause.*)
My brother's here
(*Pause.*)
Here but not here
(*Pause.*)
A man encountering the body of his father for the first time
can hardly be expected to bound up the stairs
(*Pause.*)
Such meetings if meetings they are and strictly speaking
the living and the dead cannot be said to meet meetings
such as this are rarely characterized by impatience on the
contrary a certain reluctance is appropriate a reluctance
originating in an instinct or if not in an instinct in decorum
I myself was
(*Pause.*)
Stiff hair she said
(*Pause.*)
My so-stiff hair
(*Pause.*)
I knew her hair was stiff
(*Pause.*)
My brother wore a coat presumably the coat is damp and
she has most considerately hung it from a peg
(*Pause.*)
Whilst his manners are scarcely what I would call refined
certainly my brother is capable of muttering the platitudes
occasions such as this require we are united in our grief to
take just one example the one she herself employed what
grief I
(*He suddenly stands.*)
She's naked
She's naked
(*Pause.*)
Under her coat she's naked
(*He walks wildly and stops.*)
Naked
Naked

He's not blind and lifting his damp coat from his shoulders
inevitably her own fell open was it buttoned was it belted
no oh no although it had a belt she left the coat unbelted
so as she moved it flowed like water round her thighs she's
not stupid those cruel eyes far from stupid and my brother
is not blind
(*Pause.*)
He sinks
He sinks down to the tiles
She leans
She tilts
She parts
He takes her whole cunt in his mouth the flesh the fluid
and the hair stiff hair oh such stiff hair and if she
(*A man enters and stops. His gaze falls on the body of his father.
He emits a howl of such intensity that EFF is discomforted and,
returning to his chair, sits, head in hands.*)
ISTVAN: My father
My father
(*EFF squirms.*)
My father
Oh
My father
Oh
My dear
My dear
My dear dear father
(*He sobs.*)
EFF: I've been here hours
(*Pause.*)
Not hours
(*ISTVAN goes to the body, shaking his head.*)
A vile journey
Unremittingly vile only at one point did the vileness cease
ISTVAN: (*Erupting again.*) My father
Oh my dear dear father
(*EFF stands and walks stiffly from the room. ISTVAN strug-
gles but fails to control his grief, his head shaking and his fists*

opening and closing compulsively. EFF returns and sits again.)
EFF: The road began to steam in glaring sunshine birds
    became vociferous insects swarmed I find her hands
    peculiar the hands of his mistress peculiar do you?
    (*Pause.*)
    I don't mean offensive
    (*Pause.*)
    Quite the contrary aged hands but at the same time
    infantile
    (*Pause.*)
    When she removed my coat did she do this to you I saw
    these hands exhibited against the dark material
    Small
    Eroded
    Mummified
    The girl-sized talons of a pharaoh's queen
    (*Pause.*)
    Perhaps you did not bring a coat?
ISTVAN: No
EFF: You live so near
ISTVAN: I don't have a coat
    (*Pause.*)
EFF: You don't have a coat and living near it would be sheer
    redundancy to wear it if you did have one unless to satisfy
    some lingering addiction to conventional formalities a dark
    one obviously grey black or navy blue you haven't a tie
    either I dislike ties myself
    (*Pause.*)
ISTVAN: I don't have a tie
    (*Pause.*)
EFF: Seeing these antique hands I was swept by contradictory
    and unfamiliar feelings whilst decay inevitably causes one
    to flinch in her case this repulsion was tempered and to
    some extent abolished by a powerful awareness of her
    beauty a beauty somehow severed from all considerations
    of innocence or youth yet how youthful she is how
    agile I am reminded of an animal some sure-footed
    quadruped and within the space of a single glance these

hands became imbued with mystery their slender and
reptilian decrepitude compelling me to speculate I can
speak frankly to a brother surely not only on the number
of men but also on the intimacy with which the bodies
of these men had been explored far from representing
themselves as they lay on my shoulder as the arid claws of
a prematurely aged woman they became the source and
focus of a desperate and possibly degrading sensuality I
came swiftly and powerfully erect I can speak frankly to a
brother surely I wanted her whole cunt in my mouth the
flesh the fluid and the hair stiff hair I imagined and if she
pissed so much the better

(*Pause.*)

ISTVAN: I fled

(*He looks at EFF.*)

I fled

(*Pause. EFF stands.*)

EFF: You fled

(*He shakes his head.*)

You fled and in a manner of speaking so did I how frank
one can be with a brother things impossible to confess to
others out of shame or damaged pride are readily admitted
it is as if the intimacy of the years albeit this intimacy was
frequently unwelcome and the consequence of a confined
domesticity nevertheless abolished the will to hide one's
darkest secrets she stood there naked naked but for shoes
and I

(*ISTVAN sobs loudly.*)

Impulsive as I am on this occasion I

ISTVAN: My father

I

Fled

My

Father

(*He chokes. EFF sits.*)

I fled and hid myself until he died

(*Pause.*)

EFF: Father

(*Pause.*)

Funny word

(*Pause.*)

The dilemma you describe was obviously a consequence
of your proximity whereas I living at such a distance was
unsurprised to find him dead when I arrived dead washed
and laid out as you see him now and her with these narrow
eyes haunting the hallway these razorblades these flints of
eyes I knew I'd sleep with her if not today tomorrow I

(*ISTVAN turns a tortured face towards his brother. He fights to
choke his bitterness. Pause.*)

ISTVAN: Why

Why

At the very crisis of his life did I abandon him he turned
his frightened eyes to me I stroked his darling forehead I
might have shared his ordeal with him but I lied I said I
would return I knew I never would return I lied I lied to
him who loved me with an uncritical devotion the father
of all fathers never did he injure me never did he utter a
reproving word and yet I lied I lied to him I lied

(*Pause.*)

EFF: Her decision

(*Pause.*)

Her decision to enter this room naked for all that I both
desired and predicted it nevertheless precisely was decision
decision and not spontaneity characterized her actions and
her

(*SOPRON walks in, exquisitely dressed in mourning. EFF
stands. SOPRON takes the chair. Pause.*)

ISTVAN: He would forgive me obviously he would forgive
both the betrayal and the lie but can I forgive myself?

(*Pause.*)

SOPRON: You say you have no tie but what is to stop you
buying one there is an outfitter three doors from here they
sell ties

(*Pause.*)

ISTVAN: Or is the forgiving of myself the very proposition
that I require forgiveness from any quarter let alone

myself another cruel and humiliating demonstration of my
solipsistic character my father dies my beloved father my
uncritical and devoted father dies and I whilst affecting
to grieve for him what do I do I make his death another
pretext for self-laceration self-examination self-intoxication
self self self I am so tired of self I am so sick with I this I
my I

SOPRON: Blue if you don't like black blue is acceptable
nowadays navy blue

(*Pause.*)

I have a small blue brooch here look

(*She shows a lapel.*)

I have a spray of jet but so much black can appear
excessive even contrived whereas this single discrepancy
of colour this solitary infringement of the rule if anything
reveals the depth of my

(*She stands violently.*)

Get a tie get a tie just get a tie

(*Pause. She sits. ISTVAN makes to go.*)

EFF: It cannot be that simple can it?

(*ISTVAN stops.*)

Even if the facts are as you say they are and whilst there is
no one to corroborate them all the same let us accept your
version that you cruelly betrayed your father and that this
betrayal coming as it did at the very nadir of his existence
was spectacularly pitiless and provided yet another pretext
for you to hate yourself all the same you were punishing
him albeit you loved your father profoundly nevertheless
you were inflicting a blow I say your father my father also
what a funny word when I speak it I feel nauseous

SOPRON: Tie

Tie

(*ISTVAN is undecided. He goes to leave.*)

EFF: I have one here

(*ISTVAN stops. EFF removes a black tie from his suit pocket.*)

Always I have a spare

(*He extends it to ISTVAN.*)

No there is more to this exquisite cruelty than meets the

eye
(*ISTVAN holding the tie limply in his fingers weeps. Pause.*)
SOPRON: Tie
(*ISTVAN wails. SOPRON goes to him and lifting his collar begins to dress him with the tie.*)
EFF: For all the self-aggrandizement you correctly identify
(*ISTVAN sobs.*)
My own conviction is that in your inveterate egoism you were merely the agent of another
SOPRON: Back
Head back
ISTVAN: (*His head tilted.*) What other?
EFF: The instrument of some other
ISTVAN: What?
(*He stares at EFF.*)
Of what was I the instrument?
(*Pause.*)
EFF: You resent my intervention forgive me I have intruded on your consciousness I have trodden clumsily on the perimeters only the perimeters of an exquisitely cultivated ego only the perimeters thank God
SOPRON: (*Withdrawing from ISTVAN.*) The tie is adequate
EFF: I am wearing the better of the two ties obviously the other
SOPRON: Yes
EFF: The other as I think I have explained
SOPRON: Yes
EFF: Is spare
SOPRON: Unfortunately the tie produces an effect I could never have anticipated it draws attention to the hair
EFF: Yes
SOPRON: Neatness
EFF: Is cumulative
SOPRON: Even my underwear is compatible with my outer garments the fact that elements of one's dress are destined to remain invisible is neither here nor there take off the tie take off the tie or go to a barber there is a barber's shop three doors from here

ISTVAN: (*Conforming to her instruction.*) So this ostensibly
disgusting act which I was fully prepared to spend my life
studying regretting and atoning for
(*He tugs at the tie.*)
Whilst it remains disgusting nevertheless

SOPRON: (*Standing.*) No

ISTVAN: According to you

SOPRON: (*Going to ISTVAN.*) You are making it worse

ISTVAN: Must be understood in the wider context of what
what exactly you described me as an agent very well what
was I an agent of?

SOPRON: If you have never learned to tie a tie it stands to
reason I suppose
(*She works at the knot.*)
That you will be equally ignorant of how to go about
untying one

EFF: Let me say at once

SOPRON: (*Exasperated.*) What have you done?

EFF: That in articulating my attitude to your act of cruelty
I should not for a single moment wish to deprive you
of any satisfaction that might have accrued to you from
contemplating it

ISTVAN: Thank you

SOPRON: (*Stamping her foot.*) Oh

EFF: Shame is apparently essential to our sense of order and
propriety

SOPRON: (*Stamping again.*) Ah

EFF: It is not my function to diminish it
(*SOPRON tugs. ISTVAN winces.*)

SOPRON: I'm sorry
I'm sorry

EFF: No
All I intended to suggest was this

SOPRON: (*Flouncing away.*) Do it yourself I'm not doing it
(*She sits.*)

EFF: That the perfection which characterized your
relationship with your father

SOPRON: You look silly in a tie and silly out of one

(Pause.)

EFF: Required to be I do not say this frivolously please
believe me

SOPRON: Graceless idiot

(Pause.)

EFF: Sabotaged in some way even if this act of sabotage was
delayed right up to the hour of his
*(EFF is surprised to see SOPRON rush back to ISTVAN and
smother him with kisses.)*
Death
*(ISTVAN stares at EFF. SOPRON encircles him with her arms.
Her head hangs.)*
Why should this be?
(SOPRON drifts out. Pause.)
Presumably because perfection is abhorred
(His gaze follows SOPRON.)
Not only by men
But by the laws which govern our existence
(Pause.)
To die you must I think be stricken by the poverty of
things therefore whilst your action was strictly speaking a
betrayal of a doomed and frightened man in actual fact you
rendered him a critical and final service
(Pause.)
That woman
(He turns to ISTVAN.)
You have had her whole cunt in your mouth
(Pause.)
If the world were not revealed for all its affectations as
a fatuous and sordid place how could we ever bring
ourselves to leave it no what is required above all else as
we tread so to speak the penumbra of extinction is the
affirmation that the place we are obliged to quit was in
all respects never worth inhabiting in the first place you
see you need not weep to weep in this instance is really a
misapprehension
(Pause.)
Istvan

(*Pause.*)
The flesh the fluid and the hair
(*Pause.*)
Stiff hair I imagined
(*Pause.*)
Stiff her she confirmed it
(*EFF walks a little.*)
What an arid and unlavish woman Sopron is I spoke at
some length of her shrunken hands her knifeblade of a
mouth her razor eyes but all that can be said about her
body applies perhaps more forcefully to her character her
short temper her fastidiousness with regard to etiquette
everything about her narrow hard and fenced and yet
(*Pause.*)

ISTVAN: Yes
    Yes
    (*He goes and sits in the chair.*)
    Yes
    (*He looks at the body unflinchingly.*)
    I fled him to deliver him
    Yes
    (*ISTVAN smiles.*)
    My cruelty was kindness
EFF: Certainly
ISTVAN: My selfishness was generosity
EFF: In effect
ISTVAN: Yes
    Yes
    Of course one must be cautious not to extend this principle
    to any act of
EFF: Why not?
    (*Pause.*)
ISTVAN: Because
    (*Pause.*)
    I don't know
    (*Pause.*)
    Ha
    I

(*He shrugs. He lifts his hands.*)
I don't know
I

EFF: I was careful not to describe it as a principle it is rather
a phenomenon one of those unintended ironies which
originate not in the moral but the natural sphere of course
you will continue to reproach yourself but these reproaches
are frankly insubstantial when placed in the context of
man's relation with the universe I say man I mean one
man I mean your father by which I mean my father also
father funny word your domicile being so close to theirs
contributed I imagine to the ease with which you carried
on this love affair with your father's mistress I say your
father my father also is it love however I must beware not
to ascribe love to an action which might be distinguished
by its lovelessness to take her whole cunt in your mouth
the flesh the fluid and the hair might be what I hardly dare
suggest what rage possibly rage or even yes despair despair
can manifest itself in the erotic oh yes let us never overlook
despair

(*Pause. ISTVAN gets up and goes to leave.*)
Where are you going?

ISTVAN: Home

EFF: Home home to your sordid lodging your sordid but
conveniently local lodging and you have taken leave of
him have you the man who gave you life who nourished
and adored you who never injured criticized or even issued
one reproving word this man has been consigned to the
realm of melancholy and nostalgia it took me fifteen hours
to get here what a journey what a journey oh we grieve
in different ways we all grieve differently that was your
grieving was it?

ISTVAN: Yes

(*He goes out. Pause. EFF is motionless.*)

EFF: Shame

(*Pause.*)
Shame
(*Pause.*)

What an invidious and inextinguishable commodity shame
is I call it a commodity it is it is a commodity you could
almost weigh it in the scales lend it sell it shovel it extract
it from the ground my brother far from eliminating shame
from his consciousness only moved it around the shame
he suffered from the seduction of his father's mistress
whilst temporarily smothered in the blind exhilaration of a
mischievous love affair was only waiting for an opportunity
to erupt elsewhere what was this quitting of his father but
an attempt to punish himself for an earlier offence he did
not care to acknowledge let alone apologize for
(*He goes to sit.*)
She on the other hand she marches naked up and down
the room where
(*Pause.*)
One
Son
Sits
Resolutely
Unseduced
(*Pause.*)
She won't come back
(*Pause.*)
She won't
She won't come back and even if she did she certainly
would never do so in the form in which she first appeared
no I have observed this over and over again no woman
presents herself twice identically and who can blame her
she sensed rejection she sensed an overpowering faux pas
had obliterated the supreme erotic gesture of her life to
come back now would require a
(*SOPRON enters, naked under a coat. She walks to the coffin.
She leans across it as if stricken with grief. The coat slips from her
shoulders. EFF stares.*)
My brother
He
My brother
My brother

My brother
He
My brother
He
(*EFF writhes in a paroxysm until language at last fails him.
Under his frozen but tortured gaze SOPRON is herself motionless. Pause.*)
How right you are how perfectly well-judged this
unexpected reappearance so many reasons might explain
the failure of a man to act on one occasion but the
second oh the second how many scarcely discernible but
critical factors may have been brought to bear which will
profoundly alter the outcome the temperature for example
the quality of the air I am not facetious I am overwhelmed
by admiration for a woman who dares present herself
identically on two subsequent occasions and I called you
narrow I called you hard when since I first set eyes on you
I have thought nothing but how much I want the whole
cunt of that woman in my mouth the flesh the fluid and the
hair and if she pissed so much the better
(*He goes to move to SOPRON, but stops.*)
My brother
My brother
My brother is he here?
(*She is silent. He goes nearer. He stops.*)
He is here
(*Pause.*)
Obviously my brother's here not here not in the room not
in the house perhaps I did not suppose him to be lingering
on the stair but for all that he might be absent certainly my
brother's here no distance could diminish his proximity he
sits in his room he sits in a bar he sits for all I know in the
buffet car of some great train a glass of champagne in his
hand notwithstanding that my brother's here champagne
did I say why did I say champagne champagne I think
not I plucked the word out of the air I was evoking
contemplation I was evoking meditation but my brother
and champagne it's inconceivable elegance is not the

source of his fascination I feel sure you will confirm I am
sitting I am not taking your whole cunt in my mouth I am
returning to my chair conscript another to your sordid and
(*Walking backwards EFF collides with the chair and overturns
it, falling himself in the upset. Pause.*)
Or perhaps not sordid I need not ascribe sordidity to what
may be a complex and even beautiful erotic ritual the two
of you perform I however
(*He remains on the floor, observing her.*)
I
I
I however
(*He is silent. She is still.*)
The spectacle of your nakedness you obviously think
abolishes the indignation I have been attempting to
describe it does it does go a very long way to abolishing it
(*He stares fixedly.*)
What you fail to recognize is the detrimental effect
resentment has upon all things erotic
(*Pause.*)
The tenderness associated with acts of such awesome
intimacy as suggest themselves to me is annihilated by a
sense of injured pride
(*Pause.*)
Rage
Cruelty
The antics of revenge supply the place vacated when
desire's compromised
(*Pause.*)
And still you
(*Pause.*)
You still
(*Pause.*)
Still you
(*EFF climbs off the floor. He is mesmerized by SOPRON's naked
immobility. He draws near to her.*)
I love you
I love you

Sopron
Sopron
Mistress of my Father
Mistress of my Brother
Mistress of the Multitude
Your hands are claws but oh your arse
Your lips are clay but oh your thigh
Clay dry your lips
Kicked glass your eye
Sopron
Sopron
I love you and I want to die
(*He sobs. SOPRON is quite still.*)
I do
I do
(*He seethes, shrinks, agonizes.*)
Why
Why
Why
Is my entire imagination
Not imagination
My entire intelligence
Not intelligence
The entirety of me an intellectual and the son of one an
enquiring thoughtful cultured and discriminating man not
ignorant of women and the world utterly utterly utterly
(*ISTVAN appears in the doorway.*)
Consumed by this
(*He agonizes.*)
This
(*SOPRON coolly breaks her pose and plucking up her coat walks
past ISTVAN and out.*)
He's on the train I said I said the train but I was making
the elementary mistake of confusing my instincts with
your own certainly I should have boarded a train a great
express if one happened to be standing at a platform and
with a bottle of champagne beside me watched the swiftly
changing landscape knowing my mistress was at that very

moment dark forests passing yellow fields at that very
moment children at the crossing gates at that very moment
but frankly you aren't known for spontaneous gestures of
that sort and train fares oh you hesitate to ride a bus even
if it rains you walk I describe I do not criticize I am in love
with that woman and I shall never recover from it why
should I not confide in you you are my brother if there is a
single individual
(*He stops.*)
You fled
(*Pause.*)
You fled you say
(*Pause.*)
You fled and hid where did you flee to where did you hide
oh my poor father it was her cunt you fled to her cunt was
the place in which you chose to hide
(*Pause.*)
He died alone
(*Pause.*)
He died alone my father while you father funny word
while you the two of you the two of you the two of you
(*Pause.*)
In front of him perhaps or on the stair I know little of
cruelty but cruelty I daresay does not balk at the extremes
and two have twice the cruelty two will always
(*He stops.*)
Oh
(*He shakes his head. He goes to the fallen chair and stands it on
its legs.*)
This chair
(*He contemplates it.*)
The two of you
The two of you
The two of you
A dying man
A single chair
(*Pause.*)
It would have occurred to me had I been there and I am

not a sensualist I am not a roué or a debauchee your eyes
met and the meeting of your eyes became a stare a bridge
spanning his body his suffering ceased to horrify you it
acquired the character of music an accompaniment to
exquisite nakedness what does she wear Sopron what does
she wear when a man she loves is dying do I sound bitter
no bitterness afflicts me I am an aficionado I am a devotee
of hers what clothing and her face no trace of make-up I
imagine the hair severely drawn off her
(*He stops.*)
Oh my poor father
Oh my poor father father funny word I think it must mean
sacrifice a sacrifice to what however
Us
Us
A sacrifice to us presumably if I don't fuck with Sopron
I shall kill her I have never loved a woman more in my
whole life kill her and you if necessary from the moment
her hand lay on my shoulder I knew the depth and
permanence of my servitude call her call her will you call
her here
(*ISTVAN goes out.*)
Call
Call
(*Pause.*)
Call I said but can such a woman be summoned by a call
already my brother manifests the craven disposition of a
servitude a servitude already more ingrained than mine
but then their intimacy is so much older and painful as
it is painful did I say exquisite torture as it is to me to
contemplate the style and temper of their fornication a
fornication carried on beneath the gaze of a loved and
dying man I must acknowledge no act of mine could
ever eclipse what surely was on her part anyway a divine
inspiration utterly divine at no place on the entire globe
was such an apotheosis of the erotic meditated upon let
alone
(*Pause.*)

And where was I oh I was on the road in such vile weather
unremittingly vile
(*Pause.*)
No
(*He shakes his head ruefully.*)
No it did remit on leaving somewhere this unremitting
vileness ceased the road began to steam in glaring sunshine
birds became vociferous
(*Pause.*)
The very moment she flung up her skirt
(*Pause.*)
The very moment obviously
(*He smiles bitterly. ISTVAN enters.*)
ISTVAN: She's at the dentist's
(*EFF goes to the chair and sits. Pause.*)
EFF: With or without your acquiescence I think it likely
Sopron will expose herself to me again and on the
third occasion you can be certain I shall not fail to act
so what if this renders me pitiful comic or absurd the
subject of diabolical manipulations in which she may
or may not have concurred I have been if anything too
conscious of my honour and my independence I long
to be compromised I long to be corrupted humiliated
smeared and soiled by my own appetites yes I am hardly
recognizable I am a craven supplicant who prostrates
himself at the feet of a coarse and common woman
what did my father see in her I say my father yours also
obviously father father funny word
(*Pause.*)
ISTVAN: Her teeth are not white at least not sufficiently
white for her own satisfaction this particular dentist
has a treatment for discolouration every week she goes
sometimes I do sometimes I wait and read the magazines
EFF: I envy you
ISTVAN: Not infrequently a little of the preparation hangs on
her lip I look up from the magazine and there it is
EFF: White?
ISTVAN: White powder on her lip

(*He laughs a little.*)

I have not gone this week this week I felt unable to

EFF: She however

ISTVAN: She has kept the appointment yes

(*Pause. EFF rises from the chair. He walks to the body. He gazes.*)

EFF: Strange

ISTVAN: Strange?

EFF: Strange that coming here as I did in a state of
considerable apprehension the unburied pains of
childhood the melancholy memory of adolescence the
strained and sometimes bitter conflicts of maturity all those
never to be resolved contradictions which afflict us in our
relations with our parents weighing on my conscience as
I came through the door strange I should so swiftly and
catastrophically fall in love that none of this remotely
troubles me it is as if in selecting Sopron to be his mistress
my father knew the agonies I should experience in my
encounter with his corpse would be relieved or at least
diverted by the spectacle she presented to me how wise
and perspicacious my father was not only my father yours
too of course

(*He laughs.*)

Conversely my falling so calamitously in love with
my father's mistress might be judged to have occurred
precisely to avoid this very confrontation any woman
might have played the role

(*He scoffs.*)

Her hands her hands to isolate a single element of her
entire anatomy her hands are the hands of a corpse a
mummy a long dead thing what possible attraction could a
man discover in those hands unless

(*He goes to the chair.*)

And you

The little smear of dental preparation you so lovingly
described the substance clinging to her lip what is that but
a failure of decorum yet it charms you what is Sopron?

(*Pause.*)

What is Sopron?

To you?
To me?
(*Pause.*)
She is surely and I say this with a terrible foreboding
surely nothing but misapprehension the apotheosis of the
inauthentic I do not desire her and nor do you her erotic
authority derives entirely from our inability to admit to
feelings both of us separately entertained with regard to
him the dead man on the table the man I call my father
I no more wish to take her whole cunt in my mouth than
stoop to lap a puddle from a flooded drain I say my father
yours also obviously father funny word I am lying I am
lying Istvan
ISTVAN: Yes
EFF: I do I do want to take her whole cunt in my mouth
ISTVAN: Yes
EFF: The flesh the fluid and the hair
ISTVAN: Of course you do
EFF: And if she pissed so much the better I am trying to
describe the poverty of this desire Istvan
ISTVAN: Yes
EFF: The poverty of it that's all
(*EFF holds his head in his hands.*)
ISTVAN: She fears this slight discolouration of her teeth may
be offending you
(*EFF looks up.*)
EFF: (*Bitterly.*) The contrary
ISTVAN: That's what I said I said my brother is profoundly
moved by all those things in you which conventional
society prefers to smother in embarrassment but Sopron is
conventional she will come here again of course and show
her nakedness to you repeatedly until your reluctance is
overcome in that sense she is hardly conventional at all
(*Pause.*)
EFF: Whereas I have now arrived at some vague
understanding why this decayed and petty woman
exercises such a hegemony over my soul at least
insofar as it appears to justify my failure to address the

moral and emotional chaos unleashed by my father's
death I must confess to an almost total ignorance as to the
motives of Sopron herself in making herself available so to
speak

ISTVAN: That's her

EFF: As a refuge for my moral cowardice and probably yours

ISTVAN: (*Leaving the room swiftly.*) That's her

EFF: No woman let alone one of her limited sophistication
could possibly apprehend the complexities of the
unconscious sufficiently to actually volunteer her body
for this scarcely healthy function no Sopron has her own
reasons for this extraordinary
(*SOPRON enters. She stops, looking at EFF.*)

SOPRON: Your brother is mistaken

EFF: Is he?

SOPRON: I shall not I promise you expose myself to you
again
(*EFF looks at the floor.*)
Whilst I do not in the least regret my actions I
(*Pause. She bites her lip.*)
Shall I?
(*Now she looks at the floor.*)
Shall I perform the action again I should hate it if by
declining to repeat myself a third time I forfeited the
opportunity however remote to
(*She falters.*)
How silly
(*She shakes her head.*)
How utterly silly I have manoeuvred myself into the
humiliating position of requiring you to confirm your own
participation in an action which could only be tolerable so
long as it purported to be spontaneous silly silly but was it
ever spontaneous I don't think it was
(*Pause.*)
Confirm it then
(*EFF is hesitant. SOPRON strides from the room. EFF rises to
his feet, bitter and provoked.*)

EFF: Confirm it yes confirm it and then what I am placed

under an obligation an obligation to do
(*He stops. He shrugs.*)
To do what I so desperately want to do
(*He half-laughs, half-sobs.*)
Ha
The
Oh
Ha
(*ISTVAN enters.*)
Call her
Call her
Call her please
Call Sopron
Sopron please

ISTVAN: (*Laconically.*) I think she's

EFF: (*Seizing his brother by the lapels of his suit.*) Call her I said
and if she isn't here go after her hurry hurry down the
stairs scour the streets if necessary the parks the gardens
the department stores I am sorry to belabour you but I am
not myself the journey here the unremitting vileness of the
journey here whereas you you who lives so near when did
you ever
(*He is forcing ISTVAN out the door.*)
inconvenience yourself when did you ever submit to the
requirements of another never never always you identify
your own interests your bohemian appearance belies a
pitiless and strident egoism Sopron please
(*He ejects ISTVAN. Pause.*)
I love her
I love her
I love her
And if the love is utterly degraded I don't care
And if the love destroys me I don't care
Let her spiteful petty and fatuous nature poison my life I
do not care
(*SOPRON walks smartly into the room. She goes directly to the
chair, sits, and composes herself.*)
I love you

(*Pause.*)

Whether this love originates in obfuscation evasion
procrastination or sheer cowardice I do not know nor do
I intend to make any effort whatsoever to discover I came
to grieve the grieving did not occur whatever grief existed
in me was extinguished by the most compulsive desire a
desire not inflamed by your nakedness awesome as it was
but by your hands hands which in their shrivelled and
antique appearance caused me to think of nothing but how
much I wanted your whole cunt in my mouth the flesh the
fluid and the hair abandon my brother live with me or do
not abandon him I cannot coerce you on the contrary I am
myself coerced into the most abject and exquisite servitude
let us discuss my father by all means but another day
(*SOPRON is still. A brief pause elapses. Suddenly she falls
forward and weeps, her face buried in her hands. EFF, puzzled
by her wailing, takes a few steps, stops, returns, stops. ISTVAN
enters, drawn by the sounds. EFF looks at him helplessly. They
wait, making occasional and aimless moves. At last SOPRON's
weeping ceases.*)

SOPRON: A handkerchief

(*Pause.*)

One of you?

(*They feel anxiously in their pockets.*)

A handkerchief?

(*They are crestfallen.*)

You come to a funeral and neither of you has a
handkerchief?

(*She stands.*)

A man must have a handkerchief white linen in the top
pocket if not for his own use then for occasions such as
this the conventions of society are not ridiculous it is you
who are ridiculous to think them ridiculous do you think
people have not over long periods of years hundreds
possibly refined the rules of etiquette precisely for their
practicality if there is small-mindedness in manners the
small-mindedness is yours I have one fortunately I have
one myself but how much better it would have been if you

had proffered yours
(*SOPRON removes a small ladies' handkerchief from her sleeve
and touches her cheeks with it.*)
Always you disappoint me always you fail to match my
dreams and they are small dreams god knows my dreams
are small enough to live cleanly to live quietly and in
the same place year after year be like smoke he said was
anyone less inclined to drift than me was anyone less
shaped by the passage of the air stiffness darkness formality
that's me I like to know things will be as I left them
sudden change disturbs me I loathe impulsiveness I loathe
spontaneity
(*She emits a short, strange laugh.*)
Smoke
Ha
Smoke
Ha
Stone am I and in the ground deep in and if I show my
arse to you again kiss it take my whole cunt in your mouth
the flesh the fluid and the hair if I show it if I do if I show
it again
(*She walks out.*)
EFF: I love you
   I love you
ISTVAN: Shh
EFF: I love you
ISTVAN: Shh
EFF: Why
   Why shh
   Why
ISTVAN: It's
EFF: What
   What is it
ISTVAN: It's
   (*He shrugs.*)
   Pitiful
   Embarrassing
   Absurd

EFF: Is it is it pitiful embarrassing and absurd perhaps it is
yes probably it is those things certainly a man might easily
lose sight of the true facts of a situation when immersed in
a love affair as passionate as this especially one where grief
was the condition to which he originally thought himself
most likely to be exposed thank you I appreciate your
objectivity whilst at the same time recalling to you with
an objectivity at least as powerful as yours the cruel and
terrible events that took place not so very long ago in that
on that or astride that chair oh my poor father I envy you I
envy you profoundly Istvan oh my poor father yours too of
course how pitiful was that how embarrassing how absurd
(*EFF seethes.*)
I should have done the same I should have done the same
and worse

ISTVAN: You were not here

EFF: I was not here or certainly I should have done

ISTVAN: You were on the road

EFF: A vile journey

ISTVAN: And the weather

EFF: Vile

ISTVAN: But had it not been had the sun been kindly shining
still the journey must now be judged to have been vile vile
on its own account

EFF: Certainly
I now know it was not the weather that made the journey
vile but what occurred whilst I was occupied with it I am
marrying Sopron I am flinging my entire life at her feet to
tread to spoil to desecrate let her dead hands claw ribbons
out of my face
(*He goes to leave, stops.*)
I want it
I want it lacerated Istvan
I want to stand in the ruins of my face while she torments
me with my ineptitude my social clumsiness my gaucherie
she was bristling with indignation Istvan did you see and
correctly why did I not bring a handkerchief if there is
a single item for which no man could fail to anticipate

the need when visiting the deathbed of his father that
item surely is a handkerchief perhaps I did not expect
to weep perhaps I knew that far from weeping I should
be exhilarated by the spectacle of an inconsolable and
exquisitely ill-tempered woman but is that not in itself a
most compelling reason to have furnished myself with one
(*He goes to leave the room, but stops.*)
My father
(*Pause.*)
My father
(*Pause.*)
It is important to recognize even at this relatively early
stage of our bereavement that my father
ISTVAN: My father also
EFF: Yours also yes our father may or may not have taken her
whole cunt in his mouth the flesh the fluid and the hair we
know so little what should be our attitude to this ignorance
I wonder
(*ISTVAN shrugs.*)
Perhaps you do not care
(*He shrugs again.*)
Sopron alone possesses the authority to enlighten us but no
woman speaks the truth when interrogated on the subject
of her former lovers and it is not mischief some censorship
obliterates the very details we so crave to hear perhaps
only in her senility in some deep shaded room of absence
and neglect do these intimate transactions bear scrutiny
you do care Istvan it is impossible you do not care your
affectation of indifference in this matter as in every other
fails to influence me you care profoundly please please
relinquish this
(*His hand plucks the air.*)
This
(*His hand falls.*)
Speaking for myself I care perhaps more than I expected
to
(*Pause.*)
Much more

(*Pause.*)

The spectacle of Sopron naked the manner of her nakedness the provocation of it its supreme artistry balanced as it was between spontaneity and utter calculation coming as it did on top of the peculiar and contradictory effect upon me of those hands could not have failed to stir in me or any man I daresay a desperate longing such that all considerations of her history were annihilated before they could appear but that was then

(*He walks up and down.*)

Much has altered in the brief time that has elapsed between that first instalment of her nakedness and the last oh yes oh yes the most unreflective breathless and impulsive passion must come under scrutiny at last I cannot gaze on those hands now without some gnawing sense of their earlier transactions interposing itself between my longing for possession and

(*He screws up his fists.*)

As for her arse

(*ISTVAN laughs.*)

That is a repulsive laugh

(*The laugh lingers.*)

That laugh if it is a laugh is sordid and degenerate

(*ISTVAN laughs longer.*)

I have heard some ugly laughter but never I think so squalid and

ISTVAN: You compel it

EFF: So lewd as

ISTVAN: You compel it

EFF: That which lingers like an infected sore now even on your lips

ISTVAN: Of course he took her whole cunt in his mouth of course he did

EFF: Istvan

ISTVAN: The flesh the fluid and the hair

EFF: Istvan

ISTVAN: And if she pissed so much the better

EFF: (*Moving with menace towards him.*) Istvan

ISTVAN: If she
    If she
    Never mind the if she
    Pissed she did
    (*EFF grabs ISTVAN by the neck.*)
    Did I say
    Did
    Did
    (*EFF propels ISTVAN backwards by the vehemence of his attack,*
    then suddenly releases him. He forces his own arms to his sides.
    Pause. ISTVAN nurses his throat.)
EFF: I am a liar
    I am a liar and your disgusting laugh was a rebuke to me a
    just rebuke
    (*He walks some paces, turns.*)
    Even as I phrased the form of the desire Sopron's bloodless
    hands inspired in me I was acutely aware not only that
    I could not have been the first to have articulated such
    an aspiration but that the act itself must certainly have
    occurred between her and my father was she not his
    mistress am I not my father's son but why Istvan did I
    ache to emulate my father or surpass him copy him or rob
    him of his place in his lover's memory was this malice or
    homage contempt or love I must sit down I am horrified to
    think what I how I I must sit down I
    (*EFF sits, smothering his head in his hands. Pause.*)
    Ask Sopron please to come in here
ISTVAN: It's Thursday
EFF: Thursday?
ISTVAN: Thursday she visits a friend I say friend this
    individual is not a friend but a former colleague now
    suffering from an incurable disease Sopron visits her
    she takes her things flowers biscuits there is little or no
    affection in it why go I say why go if there is no affection in
    it is it not insincere she looks at me with those narrow eyes
    you have no sense of duty she replies twelve years she has
    visited this woman twelve years apparently
    (*Pause.*)

She stays about an hour
Sometimes less
(*Pause.*)
They hardly speak
(*Pause.*)
There is a smell
(*Pause.*)
This smell clings to Sopron
(*Pause.*)
As soon as she comes in she flings off her clothes
(*Pause.*)
It clings however even to her nakedness
(*Pause.*)
It's sickness I suppose
(*Pause.*)
It's death
(*The two men look into one another for a long time.*)

EFF: My father

ISTVAN: Yes

EFF: My father
(*Pause.*)
I daresay he
(*Pause.*)
Your father too of course
(*Pause.*)
Discovered in this poisoned nakedness a source of
(*Pause. EFF stands with a violent movement. The chair falls.*)
I refuse I refuse I refuse

ISTVAN: Yes

EFF: I refuse Istvan

ISTVAN: Me too

EFF: We both refuse
(*He paces to and fro.*)

ISTVAN: Yes but

EFF: How right I was how wholly and utterly correct even not
knowing the correctness of it to deny her I was ashamed
Istvan I was humiliated I suffered the acute embarrassment
of failing to act when this failure far from being failure was

pure inspiration some instinct Istvan I don't know which some greater instinct than the instinct which compelled me to desire her deprived me of the will to act a war of instincts raged in me a war in which the right side won

(*Pause.*)

ISTVAN: Yes but

EFF: Obviously

(*Pause. He looks at ISTVAN.*)

Obviously if she repeats the act a third time I will submit

(*Pause.*)

Obviously Istvan

(*Pause.*)

I am my father's son

(*Pause.*)

ISTVAN: Me too

EFF: Both of us

(*Pause.*)

Sons of the father father funny word I think it must mean sacrifice but in what way a sacrifice?

(*EFF walks and stops.*)

Surely a willing one an ecstasy if sacrifice can be yes to be murdered by the son is ecstasy you murdered him but I might have done

(*Pause.*)

ISTVAN: I?

I?

EFF: On that chair with Sopron

(*ISTVAN is appalled.*)

As he lay dying yes you stripped her as she stood there fingers raging at the buttons or did she throw it up the dress both of you breathless she standing you sitting in the chair I don't know for certain but I am prepared to guess she tilted up her arse she opened up her thighs the father dying the son adoring his amazement her deep cries you took her whole cunt in your mouth the flesh the fluid and the hair and if she

(*Pause.*)

If she

If she
Never mind the if
So intense was the encounter she did piss
(*Pause.*)
Ecstasy Istvan to be murdered by your favourite son
(*Pause. EFF shakes his head.*)
As for my vile journey
(*He half smiles.*)
Like so much that offends us it achieves its own perfection
when viewed in retrospect
(*Pause.*)
How terrible if I had come in upon the three of you
ISTVAN: Yes
EFF: Wet and bad-tempered from that interminable road
ISTVAN: Oh yes
     (*They smile.*)
EFF: Beauty is a thing seized on a landing when ugliness is
     half-way up the stairs
     (*They laugh.*)
ISTVAN: Yes
     Yes
     But you are not ugliness
EFF: Me?
     No
     (*Pause. EFF goes, turns up the chair and sits.*)
     The appalling servitude endured by my father will
     inevitably be reproduced in me no matter how vehemently
     I proclaim my determination to avoid it we both know this
     Istvan don't we your refusal was if anything less authentic
     than my own it is a matter of time is it not the combination
     of pettiness and sensuality that characterizes Sopron will
     overcome my faltering resistance as it conquered his
     whatever our dissensions I never ceased to reverence my
     father's brilliance and originality yet these very qualities
     possibly rendered him more susceptible to her even than
     me who is neither brilliant nor original I am afraid Istvan
     look at me I am my father's son and horribly afraid
     (*He leaps off the chair.*)

She's here
She's here
(*ISTVAN swiftly leaves. EFF makes a futile move, then retracts it. SOPRON enters, stops. Pause.*)
SOPRON: I visit a woman
(*Pause.*)
This woman has an incurable disease
(*Pause.*)
Every Thursday for twelve years I do not enjoy it
(*Pause.*)
Your father's death might have licensed me to neglect what is a somewhat onerous responsibility but I am dutiful if nothing else instead I compromised compromise is typical of me I stayed only a few minutes long enough however to
(*Pause.*)
Perhaps you detect it
(*Pause.*)
The odour clinging to me?
EFF: I think so
SOPRON: Istvan runs the bath for me he waits he sees me coming up the path taps on before I've taken out the front door key I hand him my clothes he runs directly to the cleaners why not wear the same clothes for this unhealthy woman he asks me special clothes for visiting?
EFF: Impossible?
SOPRON: It would offend her the sick are far from stupid
EFF: Not only her
SOPRON: Not only she would be offended the idea offends me
(*Pause. They stare. They stir.*)
EFF: The odour
It's
SOPRON: You do not mind the odour?
(*Pause.*)
Despite the odour
(*Pause.*)
Or because of it you
(*Pause. EFF's head hangs.*)

EFF: I am my father's son
  (*Pause.*)
SOPRON: This visiting I think you know whilst it has the
  appearance of unflawed charity
EFF: I am my father's son
SOPRON: Like so much in life is replete with ambiguity on
  the one hand I
EFF: I said
  (*Pause.*)
  I said
  (*He looks cruelly at SOPRON.*)
  I am my father's son
  (*Pause.*)
  Please
  (*Pause.*)
  This talent for articulating the trivial and mundane has
  no appeal for me obviously your charity is ambiguous it
  was ambiguous in the mouth of Christ you are a shallow
  cruel and mischievous woman but my life is altered it was
  altered from the moment your hand showed starkly on the
  blue cloth of my overcoat altered and spoiled perhaps I
  love you
  (*He shakes his head.*)
  Perhaps spoiled did I say perhaps I love you my brother
  attends on you and so do I him upstairs me down Sopron I
  find it hard to breathe
  (*EFF staggers into the chair. He sits head in hands. Pause.*)
SOPRON: I'm going up
  (*She goes to leave.*)
EFF: Everything
  Is
  Proper
  (*She stops.*)
  All
  Is
  Correct
  (*Pause.*)
SOPRON: I know

EFF: My reluctance
   My cowardice
   My squirming
   And my rage
SOPRON: Yes
EFF: Proper
   And
   Correct
SOPRON: Yes
   (*SOPRON goes out. EFF suddenly stands.*)
EFF: The word love I cannot help noticing is one which
   never crosses Sopron's lips if ever man lent woman the
   opportunity to speak the word then that was it indeed I will
   admit much of what I said myself was designed precisely
   to permit this word to be uttered I say permit I coaxed the
   word I beckoned it still she declined
   (*Pause.*)
   I on the other hand have spoken it too often possibly I
   have damaged it one can oh yes one can diminish words
   by too frequent repetition and not only words the thing
   itself is equally susceptible Sopron perhaps speaks this
   word very rarely or
   (*He stops pacing.*)
   Never at all
   (*He looks to the coffin.*)
   Oh
   My
   Poor
   Father
   (*ISTVAN enters, SOPRON's suit over his arm.*)
   Does she?
   Does she ever say the word?
ISTVAN: The word?
EFF: Love
   Does she say it ever?
ISTVAN: Love?
EFF: The word the word love yes
ISTVAN: (*Pondering.*) I

EFF: No

> It's obvious the word has never passed her lips not with
> him with you not anyone it is a further aspect of her
> shrunken shrivelled and suffocated personality that
> (*He gestures wildly.*)
> I say it all the time I say it and she
> (*He lifts an empty hand.*)
> She does not say it she has no intention of saying it quite
> possibly she cannot say it
> Or
> Or
> Or
> Yes
> She cannot feel it she cannot feel it and therefore cannot
> say it even if she wanted to even as a condescension an
> act of pity or a tasteless joke no she cannot pass the word
> between her teeth
> (*EFF stares at ISTVAN.*)
> I am
> In precisely the same way my father was both exhilarated
> and enslaved
> (*Pause.*)

ISTVAN: I have dry-cleaning

EFF: I say my father yours too of course

> (*Pause.*)
> Deliver the dry-cleaning Istvan
> (*ISTVAN leaves. EFF goes to the chair. He sits. A pause. SO-
> PRON, naked beneath a coat, enters. She looks at EFF, delib-
> erately. She seems to breathe uneasily. With decision, she goes to
> walk to the dead man, EFF jumps to his feet.*)
> No
> (*SOPRON stops.*)

SOPRON: I must

EFF: No

SOPRON: I must grieve who are you to stop me grieving

> (*SOPRON glares at EFF.*)

EFF: (*Conceding.*) Grieve yes

SOPRON: My grief does not require permission

EFF: (*Going to leave.*) Grieve I said

SOPRON: (*Stung.*) I will I will grieve I will grieve for you as well as for myself since you came here what grieving have you done where are the smallest signs of your bereavement there are none

(*She glares at EFF. EFF frowns, unable to leave. SOPRON sobs through her anger, then with a single movement, flings herself across the dead man's coffin allowing her coat to fall precisely as on the previous occasions. EFF gazes at her nakedness as her cries of grief shake SOPRON's body. Tenderness and desire draw him slowly towards her. He picks her coat off the floor, drapes her with it and draws her whole body into his arms. SOPRON is unresisting as EFF carries her sobbing from the room, passing ISTVAN who, returning, steps aside as they pass. ISTVAN is still. At last he goes to the chair. He sits. He adjusts his clothing, anxiously. Suddenly he stands again, calling.*)

ISTVAN: I'll cut my hair

(*There is no reply.*)

I should have gone in when I came back from the cleaners

(*Pause.*)

I passed the barber's there was no one there

(*He does not move.*)

Silly

(*Pause.*)

When I go back the shop will be

(*Pause.*)

Oh

(*Pause.*)

Swarming not a single chair available that is so often the case with barber's shops quite inexplicable even they the barbers find it puzzling it is as if whole classes trades streets regiments discover from some faint movement of the air an overpowering requirement for a haircut they tumble over one another they jam the door and the barber oh his scissors oh his till ring snip ring

(*Pause.*)

No

(*Pause.*)

Silly
(*Pause.*)
Silly to go now
(*Pause. Then he laughs loudly and oddly. EFF enters. ISTVAN stands, vacating the chair. EFF sits. Pause.*)
EFF: I took her whole cunt in my mouth the flesh the fluid and the hair stiff hair as I anticipated and when she pissed it was
(*Pause.*)
Certainly it was
(*Pause.*)
So much the better
(*SOPRON walks smartly into the room, stiffly dressed, immaculate in mourning.*)
SOPRON: I have a train to catch
(*The brothers stare.*)
My sense of order and propriety which both amuses and enrages you forbids me to attend the funeral a pity possibly but inhibition generates a beauty of its own what is more beautiful than the march of two sons to a father's grave two sons alone I have a brother who will meet me do you know I have not left this place for years the station where is the station I was obliged to ask I had no
EFF: Shh
SOPRON: Not the least idea
EFF: Shh
SOPRON: No
EFF: Shh
SOPRON: No
EFF: There is no station here
SOPRON: No station?
EFF: Shh
SOPRON: No station?
EFF: Shh
SOPRON: No station here?
(*She closes her eyes. Pause.*)
All the same I have a ticket
(*She turns on her heel and goes to stride from the room. In*

the doorway she stops. Her body seems to collapse. Her hand reaches…)

ISTVAN: I'll collect the cleaning

(*SOPRON's hand gropes.*)

SOPRON: And visit the barber

ISTVAN: I was saying only just now I had let the perfect opportunity slip by how rarely do you see a barber's shop with empty chairs

SOPRON: Queue

ISTVAN: I shall have to I expect

SOPRON: Queue

ISTVAN: Yes I will need to now

(*He does not leave. They are all still.*)

EFF: No station and to issue you a ticket was a cruel deception the mischievous humour of a provincial mind which cannot contemplate a woman of your quality without desiring to humiliate her nevertheless my father chose to domicile himself precisely here perhaps provincial humour gratified him give me the ticket I will dispose of it the sophisticated even the barely sophisticated require resources both of patience and contempt to survive in such an atmosphere the ticket please

(*EFF extends a hand to SOPRON. She does not proffer a ticket. Pause.*)

The ticket in order that I may

(*SOPRON is still. EFF's hand falls abruptly.*)

Strange

Strange the intensity of this feeling I am obviously in the grip of some terrible apprehension that the ticket represents something injurious to me your free will for example your ability to desert my life when you have so completely taken charge of it the ticket threatens me and the fact that there is no longer a station hardly relieves the pain of it the ticket please the ticket Sopron I love you give me the ticket

(*Pause.*)

SOPRON: Yes

(*Pause.*)

Yes

(*Pause.*)

EFF: You acknowledge that your continuing possession of the
ticket is an obstacle to

SOPRON: Yes

EFF: The fullest consummation of our passion
notwithstanding I have only minutes ago taken your whole
cunt in my mouth

SOPRON: Yes

EFF: The flesh the fluid and the hair

SOPRON: I acknowledge it yes

EFF: You acknowledge it and yet you

SOPRON: Yes

(*She turns desperately to ISTVAN.*)

The cleaning

The cleaning and the barber

I tell you I remind you I nag and gnaw and intimidate you
and when I turn around you are still there

(*She turns back to EFF.*)

The ticket

The ticket

Yes

(*And back to ISTVAN.*)

Go

Go when I say

(*And back to EFF again.*)

The ticket is

(*ISTVAN goes swiftly to SOPRON and putting a hand firmly
over her mouth draws her squirming towards the chair. By su-
perior strength he forces her into a sitting position and fixes her
there. EFF watches this. SOPRON becomes still.*)

EFF: How correct you are to keep the ticket how correct to
leave me in a state of fear no matter how unqualified your
utterances still you demonstrate the possibility that our
union is frail vulnerable illusory I must struggle always
with the spectre of a devastating loss even in the most
passionate embraces sense the proximity of flight betrayal
degeneration and the station whilst closed now might well

open again the rails were not lifted I understand and the
signal box is regularly maintained don't abandon me don't
don't abandon me don't Sopron don't
(*Pause.*)
I cannot know how greatly my father loved you I can only
assert I love you more is that a contradiction if it is I do not
flinch from it it is a contradiction yes it is so what so what
(*He laughs.*)
ISTVAN: I'll join the queue
EFF: Join it yes
ISTVAN: And if it straggles round three corners
EFF: Nevertheless
ISTVAN: I'll join it
(*ISTVAN goes out. A long pause elapses, whilst EFF contem-
plates SOPRON. She gazes at the floor.*)
EFF: You spoke
(*Pause.*)
As I lay with your whole cunt in my mouth you spoke
(*Pause.*)
Words not utterances a sentence not a cry but situated as
I was my head between your thighs I could not discern
the meaning and besides even to hear seemed a breach
of manners why would a man so haunted by a passion to
be there and nowhere else on earth there there among the
flesh the fluid and the hair of his adored one care what she
muttered all the same you spoke
(*Pause.*)
In measured tones
(*Pause.*)
Unfaltering
(*Pause.*)
As if reading from a card
(*Pause.*)
In a courtroom
(*Pause.*)
Or an optician's shop
(*Pause.*)
And then this warm cascade of piss

Please
Tell
Me
This
Was
Not
Ordinary
(*SOPRON is motionless. EFF walks a few paces. He stops. He laughs, but ironically.*)
It was ordinary
It was
It was
It was ordinary
(*Suddenly he goes to the body of his father and in a surge of despair weeps.*)
My father
Oh
Oh
My father
Father help your little boy
Father
Funny word
(*EFF sobs.*)

SOPRON: Don't weep
(*EFF silences himself.*)
The dignity of a man consists in his not yielding to his feelings however natural those feelings are that is the paradox of dignity dignity presumes grief it does not advertise grief

EFF: Yes

SOPRON: Let us from this moment on abstain from all those manifestations of emotional excitement that are commonly described as natural

EFF: Yes

SOPRON: Learning stillness and speaking fewer words

EFF: Yes

SOPRON: How can freedom know itself unless freedom is confined?

EFF: I don't know

SOPRON: The thing that recently occurred between us was
not ordinary quite the contrary as for the words you heard
me utter and the way in which I uttered them darling I
held the world behind them I held the world behind four
words darling may I call you darling darling may I

EFF: What words?

SOPRON: Four common words

EFF: What words?

SOPRON: Words of no significance

EFF: Sopron

SOPRON: I called you darling

EFF: Speak the words

SOPRON: To call you darling is not a simple matter for me

EFF: Sopron

SOPRON: Nakedness came easier

EFF: Sopron

SOPRON: Nakedness is not the revelation that darling is

EFF: (*Insistent.*) The words

SOPRON: Darling

EFF: The words

SOPRON: Darling
(*Pause. SOPRON gazes on EFF.*)

EFF: I am never to know the words the four words that you
uttered never to know and if I beat you you would invent
four others and if I pleaded nagged and pestered you for
seven years seven years in which I was your darling when
you pitied me sufficiently to speak them I would shrink
with disappointment surely I would say surely those cannot
be the words no it is better these four words lie rotting in
the catacombs of secrecy that gape beneath our marriage
much better say the words Sopron say the words that your
passion swept into fragments the words that were frail as
match wood in the torrent of your piss say
(*She is adamant. EFF exchanges a long stare with her. At last
he yields. His gaze falters. ISTVAN enters.*)

ISTVAN: He was taken ill
The barber

I was the ninth or tenth man in the queue
Suddenly there was a silence
The barber had gone strangely still his comb and scissors
in the air nobody moved but in the mirror we observed
his face change colour from its natural white to red and
then to blue he staggered to the door and turned the sign
around we understood his meaning and without speaking
we withdrew me first we withdrew in the order in which
we had arrived the last man called a doctor
(*Pause.*)
Peculiar
(*Pause.*)
Unpredictable
(*Pause.*)
Disconcerting and the consequence is that my hair is still
EFF: Istvan
ISTVAN: My hair remains
EFF: Istvan
(*ISTVAN is silent.*)
Whilst not wishing to diminish the sense of wonder that
surrounds your every transaction with the world I have to
inform you that speaking for myself all that occurs outside
this room whether of a trivial or catastrophic nature is
frankly meaningless to me an irritation an irrelevance
a fatuous diversion from the single subject that wholly
and exclusively preoccupies and possibly erodes my life
namely the soul and body of this woman if the sun died
and plunged the earth into eternal darkness it would
not cause me a moment of reflection except insofar as
it deprived me of the light by which her face and flesh
could be examined I am ill Istvan I am ill ill ill Istvan find
another barber or cut your hair yourself
SOPRON: There is a barber on the forecourt of the railway
station
EFF: There is no railway station
SOPRON: What was formerly the railway station I have seen
the pole a red and white pole
ISTVAN: That is certainly the barber's sign I wonder however

if in view of the sudden and possibly fatal sickness which
afflicted the local barber there is not something tactless or
indecent in hurrying immediately to seek the services of a
second barber who for all we know might have been the
poor man's most serious competitor

SOPRON: Not at all

ISTVAN: You don't think so?

SOPRON: I don't think so at all it is the obligation of the
barber to cut hair if he fails to cut hair his customers will
transfer their loyalty elsewhere are you supposed to go
about unshaven and unshorn for months on end while he
enjoys his convalescence obviously one pities him but pity
is neither here nor there hurry Istvan or the queue at the
second barber's shop will be longer than the queue was at
the first news travels quickly

> (*Pause.*)

ISTVAN: Yes

> Yes
>
> (*Pause.*)
>
> Yes I'll go
>
> (*He goes to leave.*)

EFF: Her hands

> (*ISTVAN stops.*)
>
> Her perished hands
>
> Her perished hands and razor eyes what are these but
> the manifestations of a savage character which I in a rare
> moment of idealism chose to ignore?
>
> (*SOPRON rises to leave.*)
>
> And not simply ignore but in a paroxysm of perversity
> chose to make the object of desire a desire so compelling
>
> (*SOPRON starts to leave.*)
>
> Sopron do not go
>
> (*She stops.*)
>
> That even with her whole cunt in my mouth the flesh
> the fluid and the hair I followed with my eyes the lightly
> clenched fists rise and fall
>
> (*SOPRON goes to move.*)
>
> Sopron do not go

(She stops.)

Until they lay like artefacts upon the pillow clenched and unclenched my father's hands were beautiful their elegance expressed his character and yet he worshipped these he worshipped her dead hands not only my father yours also
(EFF walks to SOPRON.)

Arrange your hands
(SOPRON looks at EFF.)

Arrange I said
(She is afraid yet defiant.)

These bloodless relics of antiquity and Istvan watch
(Pause, then SOPRON lays her hand on the left shoulder of her own black dress. EFF watches intently. Pause.)

The other
(SOPRON lays her second hand on the shoulder off EFF's black suit. He is exhilarated.)

Yes
(SOPRON laughs.)

Yes

Yes
(Her laughter stops.)

SOPRON: For years I hid these hands

EFF: A woman would

SOPRON: A girl

EFF: A girl would

SOPRON: Wearing gloves or folding them behind me

EFF: Yes

SOPRON: The suits I wore had pockets

EFF: Yes

SOPRON: Or if they had no pockets I took them to a dressmaker

EFF: She added pockets

SOPRON: She added pockets both in the skirt and in the jacket I was in such an agony of shame I contemplated maiming them I contemplated thrusting my hands in machines farm machines machines in factories reapers balers guillotines and following the amputations I should have chosen perfect hands in porcelain or glass I did not understand the world I did not understand how I required these shrivelled hands to show my arse three times I showed my arse

EFF: Yes

SOPRON: Life

Death

Death

Life

EFF: Yes

SOPRON: Do as I say

EFF: Yes

SOPRON: Be as I want

EFF: Yes

SOPRON: My tempers

EFF: Yes

SOPRON: Serve them

EFF: Yes

SOPRON: (*Turning to ISTVAN.*) Get out

Get out

Get out

(*ISTVAN runs out. Pause.*)

How fearful are you?

(*Pause.*)

Darling

Darling

Are you full of fear?

(*EFF nods.*)

And should it not be fearful is marriage not a thing of fear I also have fear I fear you will be less than I anticipate I fear the poverty of you I am nothing but being nothing I require you to be more do you know how terribly the poor in spirit ache to serve the deep souls I dread your little depth I dread it

(*SOPRON bites her lip in her anxiety.*)

EFF: And he?

(*She is silent.*)

And he?

(*SOPRON only returns his gaze.*)

Oh my poor father he
(*Pause.*)
It kills
(*Pause.*)
It killed him
(*Pause.*)
It killed him and it will kill me
(*SOPRON walks from the room. Pause. EFF is galvanized.*)
Good
Dead
Good
Good
All desire leads to passivity the rage and then the silence
how else could it be she however she
(*He stops.*)
Already I want her whole cunt in my mouth
(*Pause.*)
Already
(*A horror overtakes him. He is utterly still. ISTVAN walks in.
He observes EFF's stillness. He becomes himself still. At last
EFF speaks.*)
I am leaving Istvan
(*Pause.*)
I shall not see my father buried please forgive me I say my
father yours also obviously
(*Pause.*)
I love Sopron and she loves me this love however will
drain the moisture from my bones she is magnificent she
knows the secret of desire and how to keep desire from
expiring in the blankets of a fond and tepid domesticity
Father
Father
Funny word I think it must mean sacrifice
His own
His own
Surely?
(*Pause.*)
ISTVAN: I was halfway to the station when I met coming

in the opposite direction one of the customers from
the barber's shop not the barber's shop on the station
concourse but the one in which the barber had fallen ill
fatally it now appears this man had been sitting next to me
when the attack occurred he recognized me and guessed
my destination never previously had we exchanged a
word but sickness and similar disasters loosen the strings
of manners he said no sooner had the second barber heard
the sad news relating to the first than he closed his own
shop as a mark of sympathy so I returned Sopron will be
furious but I am not to blame am I?
(*Pause.*)

EFF: (*Pointing to the table.*) The man we call our father let us
honour him in this single way Istvan that we repudiate
the humiliating aspect of ourselves that is inextricably
bound up in the desire we feel for a woman whose beauty
is itself inextricably connected to her ugliness her pride
her anger her hands her arse whilst it is true I already long
to take her whole cunt in my mouth notwithstanding it is
only minutes since I did precisely that I am certain that
my father is however silent nevertheless urging on me my
escape I say my father yours also obviously dear man the
dear dear man never have I felt such a proximity to him
our souls are so to speak in a shuddering embrace I am
going I am going I am going Istvan
(*Pause. EFF does not move.*)

ISTVAN: I will tell her

EFF: You will?

ISTVAN: There is nothing to be gained by attempting to
conceal it

EFF: No

ISTVAN: How long could it be concealed for anyway?

EFF: (*Puzzled.*) I don't know

ISTVAN: Any alteration in the style or colour of one's hair is
instantly discernible if she rages at me I will point out the
facts of the situation not that the facts have ever interested
Sopron most likely she will grab a pair of scissors and hack
my hair herself I say hack she is skilful when she wants

to be it depends entirely on her mood probably not hack
we'll see
(*ISTVAN goes to leave.*)
EFF: I'm leaving Istvan
(*ISTVAN pauses, then goes out.*)
I am
I am
I am
I must tell you I resent your
(*He hurries to the door.*)
Istvan
Istvan
(*He closes his eyes in repressed anger.*)
Profoundly resent the implication that I am unable or
unwilling to carry through my stated intention I am not
like you I am if anything the contrary to you no woman
would take scissors to my hair unless she were invited to
no woman
(*Pause.*)
I am going
(*Pause.*)
Istvan has at least dispensed with rancour it is not I think
fraternal sympathy that makes it possible to admire albeit
reluctantly his utter spinelessness no he finds a subtle
pleasure in it he was smiling I believe at the prospect of
Sopron's indignation that in itself must be a warning to me
and an exhortation to
(*Pause.*)
She is naked
(*Pause.*)
Sopron is naked and he
(*Pause.*)
I am going
(*EFF hesitates, then with a swift turn hurtles towards the table
and beats the coffin with his fists.*)
How could you
Monster
How could you expose your little boy to such a vile vile

journey
A letter might have saved me
A letter of two words
In ink blood or saliva
Stay away
The redemption of a never satisfactory paternity
Stay away
The dying are capable of such exertions yes they are
propped on their pillows by the failing light of their last
day their emaciated fingers crawl over the page my adored
boy stay away
In
Ink
Blood
Or
Saliva
Stay
Away
(*Pause. EFF is still.*)
My own son when I am stricken will receive my final letter
in which I will say light candles uncork the oldest of your
clarets and dine your way through my disaster
(*He smiles.*)
My son?
(*He shrugs.*)
Sopron is past child-bearing age
(*Pause. He covers his face with his hands.*)
Oh
Oh
Oh
(*He weeps. He staggers.*)
Oh
(*His hands lift for expression.*)
ISTVAN: (*Entering.*) Not gone?
(*EFF makes a gesture of futility.*)
Sopron was not angry not in the least angry either with me
or the world there was a quality of patience in her almost
one might say of resignation

(*Pause.*)
I have seen her in this state before
(*Pause.*)
Briefly
(*Pause.*)
Only briefly
(*Pause.*)
It is as if she recognized the inexorable and
incontrovertible character of the situation and haughtily
haughtily it goes without saying haughtily conceded to it
(*Pause.*)
This is a mood which does not last
(*He chuckles. Pause.*)

EFF: In choosing not to send a letter to me
A letter even of two words
In
Ink
Blood
Or
Saliva
My father guaranteed his legacy would settle on his heir
(*Pause.*)
I am the heir
(*Pause.*)
Sopron is the legacy
(*Pause.*)
A legacy as you are probably aware cannot be refused
(*Pause.*)
I do not in any case wish to refuse it
(*Pause.*)
The personality of Sopron severe and brittle as it is perhaps
will act as a corrective to my pliable and accommodating
character just as her bigotry might modify my tolerance I
am too tolerant sometimes I think I tolerate what I am too
idle to criticize no Sopron will influence me profoundly
over the coming years I am certain of it
(*Pause.*)
My father's wisdom in discerning this combined with his

confidence that in placing her skeletal and desiccated hand
upon my shoulder his mistress would become the object
of an insatiable passion on my part testify to a subtle and
magnanimous mind I grieve I never knew him better in
death he has acquired a character of such
(*He stops. He shakes his head.*)
beauty Istvan I
(*He shakes his head. He wails, recovers. His hands wave futilely
in the air.*)
Sopron is right a man without a handkerchief is absurd
(*He sniffs.*)
Always
Ha
Always she is right
(*He wipes his eyes with the back of his hand.*)
Always
Always
Darling
Always right
(*He laughs mildly, affectionately.*)
Never again will I walk even to the shops without a
handkerchief
(*He laughs again.*)
How my father loved me Istvan
Even as you blasted his dying stare with that sublime and
terrifying mischief even as his adored one hoisted her skirts
for you to take her whole cunt in your mouth the flesh the
fluid and the so-stiff hair he knew oh with what confidence
he knew your brother and not you would be the heir to
that exquisite property
(*They look deeply.*)
I cannot share Sopron
(*Pause.*)
Launder her clothes run her baths by all means but her
nakedness from now is reserved to me the encounter I
have just described whilst it can never be obliterated from
my mind will no doubt fade as mercifully as photographs
are spoiled by sunlight so what if Istvan took her whole

cunt in his mouth I'll say am I to be driven mad by the
evocation of it am I to persecute a woman I adore for
participating in an action that occurred before she had set
eyes on me no not at all all that hurts eventually is history
will you continue to live here or look for another place this
is scarcely the city for a young man with ambition lacking
as it does even a railway station but you are not ambitious
(*EFF looks coolly at ISTVAN. Pause.*)

ISTVAN: No

EFF: No?

ISTVAN: I am not ambitious and Sopron has already
indicated that the depth of feeling she entertains for you
makes any continuation of our intimacy even of that
relatively innocent kind that has characterized it until now
impossible

(*Pause.*)

I am certain that is the explanation for her uncharacteristic
placidity when I confessed my failure to discover a barber
willing or able to cut my hair she is indifferent to me you
are the sole subject of her life it has been awesome to
witness her pathetic manoeuvres as she squirms to conceal
this from herself buying invalid train tickets to take just
one example yes awesome yet simultaneously a privilege
that my own brother could inspire passion in a woman so
severe as Sopron is moved me notwithstanding it was I
who had seduced her in the first place and in that shameful
moment shared with her an act that can never be forgotten
not by either of us as you say

(*Pause. Their cold regard remains.*)

Possibly my attendance at the funeral is under the
circumstances you describe hardly

EFF: Attend by all means

ISTVAN: Desirable I

EFF: Very well leave now Istvan leave now your instinct for
evasion is one you have no doubt correctly come to trust
Sopron and I you can be perfectly assured will make of the
occasion something dignified and proper and I shall not
fail to take if not to use my handkerchief

(*EFF creates a frigid smile. They hesitate. Suddenly EFF degenerates.*)
Oh
Istvan
Oh
Istvan
(*EFF looks pitifully at his brother.*)
The
(*He cannot articulate.*)
The
(*He shakes his head, defeated. ISTVAN holds EFF by the shoulder. EFF recovers.*)
How I admire your idle character Istvan whilst finding it incomprehensible I sense you know nothing of ecstasy but correspondingly nothing of melancholy either you will live to be old much older than me please bury me whether or not we have communicated in the meantime I should like you to be present only you Sopron and I will not have children only you only you now go and with my fraternal blessing
(*The brothers clasp one another. ISTVAN goes out. EFF is perfectly still. Pause.*)
He has gone upstairs
(*Pause.*)
Not downstairs
(*Pause.*)
Not downstairs to the door at least not yet in some minutes possibly he will go down at the moment however he is upstairs is he fetching something how can he be what is there to fetch his clothes his miserable possessions are not in this house
(*Pause.*)
He is taking leave of Sopron
(*Pause.*)
Whereas under normal circumstances Istvan lacks manners of the most rudimentary sort he now displays a scrupulous
(*He stops.*)
No

No

He must he must how could he not make some clumsy
effort at an adieu she is perhaps delaying him with anxious
and possibly impertinent enquiries as to his financial
situation his eating habits whether he has a proper overcoat
Sopron would Sopron would want to protect a young man
so apparently neglectful of himself as Istvan is
(*Pause.*)
Such enquiries cannot however take so long as this
(*Pause.*)
Can they?
(*Pause.*)
And the silence is peculiar a peculiarly studied silence it is
as if
(*Pause.*)
Even when one cannot discern a conversation in a house
there is a sense of a vocal animation possibly a drone so
low in pitch we hardly register its existence but in this case
(*EFF makes a sudden move and stops.*)
He has her whole cunt in his mouth
(*His eyes close in his ordeal.*)
The silence is precisely that form of silence which
(*He squirms.*)
Oh yes
(*He creates a terrible smile.*)
A silence of stopped breath she has her fist between her
teeth and he
(*Pause.*)
Or possibly a handkerchief
Yes
She thrusts a handkerchief between her lips and he
He
He
(*He writhes. He turns to the table. He places his hands on the
coffin.*)
Inheriting the property of one's father one inherits both
the pride and agony of it one is simultaneously privileged
and punished so to speak the legacy oh the legacy is not
without entailment entailment is that not the proper term

Sopron what a cruel gift I thank you what a cruel gift thank
you thank you now they laugh
(*He is still. The sound of laughter above.*)
A laughter which
(*He shakes his head in his bemusement.*)
Like the silence
Ha
Is peculiar to this exquisite misdemeanour
(*He listens acutely.*)
They plan a further meeting
Not soon
A little longing must ferment
(*He strains.*)
The stairs
The laughter and the stairs
His hand on her arse every step of the descent
(*He is stretched on imagination.*)
The door
(*He yearns on his toes.*)
Some rearrangement of her dress
(*Pause.*)
And
(*SOPRON enters. EFF bursts into an uncanny laugh, shaking
his head and bent nearly double by the force of it. SOPRON is
repulsed by the spectacle.*)
We know
We know
Always we know and always you bathed in an insufferable
complacency persist in the delusion we do not know it is
I daresay the most ancient of all the human ironies Rome
Greece Egypt the smoky caves of the Neanderthals the
same exquisite affectations the same faith in the power of
the lie we know however
(*EFF shakes his head, a smile lingering.*)
I say we
SOPRON: What lie?
EFF: My father and I perhaps cannot be properly described
    as we
SOPRON: What lie?

EFF: Him being dead and I
SOPRON: What lie is this?
> (*Pause, EFF looks coolly at SOPRON.*)
EFF: Not yet dead certainly
> (*Pause.*)
> All the same he communicates an excruciating satisfaction
> so tangible to me it might almost be said we
SOPRON: I never lie
> (*She fixes him with a stare.*)
> He begged me to
> (*Pause.*)
> And so will you
> (*Pause.*)
> I never lie however
> (*Pause. Her gaze is unfaltering.*)
> Demand the truth and I will give it to you
> (*Pause.*)
> You don't demand
> (*Pause.*)
> You don't demand
> (*EFF's gaze falters.*)
> You don't
> (*SOPRON laughs. Half-hysterically, and turns to stalk from the
> room. Suddenly she turns on her heel.*)
> Darling
> Darling
> Darling
> (*Her eyes close in her desperation.*)
> Darling
> Darling
EFF: Yes
SOPRON: Darling
> Darling
EFF: Yes
> (*Pause. Neither has moved. SOPRON recovers. She is still, then
> she walks out. Pause.*)
> What a journey
> (*He sits in the chair.*)
> Vile

A vile journey but the vileness was the reason I think in
retrospect the very reason I completed it the vileness was
indistinguishable from its significance obviously I might
have
(*He stops. He is quite still.*)
Stopped
Stopped reflected and turned around but what is obvious
to me now
(*Pause.*)
I did not I did not turn around

v

HOWARD BARKER

www.ingramcontent.com/pod-product-compliance
Ingram Content Group UK Ltd.
Pitfield, Milton Keynes, MK11 3LW, UK
UKHW020727280225
455688UK00012B/548